Schaefer, Lola
M.,
 We need
farmers

We Need Farmers

by Lola M. Schaefer

Consulting Editor: Gail Saunders-Smith, Ph.D.

Consultant: Tammy Huber
Member Education Coordinator
North Dakota Farmers Union

Pebble Books

an imprint of Capstone Press
Mankato, Minnesota

Pebble Books are published by Capstone Press
151 Good Counsel Drive, P.O. Box 669, Mankato, Minnesota 56002
http://www.capstone-press.com

2 3 4 5 6 7 07 06 05 04 03 02

Library of Congress Cataloging-in-Publication Data
Schaefer, Lola M., 1950–
    We need farmers/by Lola M. Schaefer.
    p. cm.—(Helpers in our community)
    Includes bibliographical references and index.
    Summary: Simple text and photographs present farmers and their role in the
community.
    ISBN 0-7368-0390-4 (hardcover)
    ISBN 0-7368-8590-0 (paperback)
    1. Agriculture—Juvenile literature. 2. Farmers—Juvenile literature. [1. Farmers
2. Occupations.] I. Title. II. Series: Schaefer, Lola M., 1950– Helpers in our
community.
S519.S32 2000
630′.922—dc21   99-19410

Note to Parents and Teachers

The Helpers in Our Community series supports national social
studies standards for units related to community helpers and
their roles. This book describes and illustrates farmers and how
they help people. The photographs support early readers in
understanding the text. The repetition of words and phrases
helps early readers learn new words. This book also introduces
early readers to subject-specific vocabulary words, which are
defined in the Words to Know section. Early readers may need
assistance to read some words and to use the Table of Contents,
Words to Know, Read More, Internet Sites, and Index/Word List
sections of the book.

Table of Contents

Some farmers grow crops.

Crop farmers
grow vegetables.

Crop farmers grow fruit.

Crop farmers grow grain.

Crop farmers use machines to plant and harvest crops.

Some farmers
raise animals.

Dairy farmers milk cows.

Poultry farmers
gather eggs.

Farmers produce most
of the food we eat.

Words to Know

dairy farmer—a farmer who raises cows that produce milk; milk can be made into butter, cheese, and yogurt.

fruit—the fleshy, juicy product of a plant; grapes, apples, and strawberries are fruit.

grain farmer—a farmer who grows plants such as wheat, corn, oats, or rye

harvest—to gather a crop

poultry farmer—a farmer who raises birds such as chickens, turkeys, or geese; poultry farmers raise poultry for their eggs and meat.

produce—to make or grow something

raise—to look after young animals until they are grown; farmers raise animals for meat, eggs, and milk.

vegetables—plants grown to be used as food; potatoes, carrots, and peas are vegetables.

Read More

Flanagan, Alice K. *A Visit to the Gravesens' Farm.* Our Neighborhood. New York: Children's Press, 1998.

Ready, Dee. *Farmers.* Community Helpers. Mankato, Minn: Bridgestone Books, 1997.

Saunders-Smith, Gail. *The Farm.* Field Trips. Mankato, Minn.: Pebble Books, 1998.

Internet Sites

Agriculture for Your Classroom
http://collections.ic.gc.ca/agriculture/home.htm

Kids Corner
http://www.ohiocorn.org/kids

Kids Farm
http://www.kidsfarm.com/wheredo.htm

Index/Word List

animals, 15
cows, 17
crop, 5, 7, 9, 11, 13
dairy, 17
eat, 21
eggs, 19
farmers, 5, 7, 9, 11,
   13, 15, 17, 19, 21
food, 21
fruit, 9
gather, 19

grain, 11
grow, 5, 7, 9, 11
harvest, 13
machines, 13
milk, 17
plant, 13
poultry, 19
produce, 21
raise, 15
use, 13
vegetables, 7

Word Count: 45
Early-Intervention Level: 9

Editorial Credits

Karen L. Daas, editor; Abby Bradford, Bradfordesign, Inc., cover designer;
   Kimberly Danger, photo researcher

Photo Credits

AGStockUSA/Thomas Dodge, cover
David F. Clobes, 14, 18
Index Stock Imagery/David R. Frazier, 6; Inga Spence, 10; Ed Lallo (1996), 12
International Stock/Uli Degwert, 8
Photo Network/Tom McCarthy, 20
Photri-Microstock/D&I MacDonald, 16
Richard Hamilton Smith, 1
Shaffer Photography/James L. Shaffer, 4